Alexander Ostrovsky

Ostrovsky (1823-1886) was born into a merchant family in Russia. He wrote 40 prose and 8 verse plays. His acknowledged masterpieces are *The Storm* (1860) and *The Forest* (1871).

Frank McGuinness

Frank McGuinness was born in Buncrana, Co. Donegal, and now lives in Dublin and lectures in English at University College, Dublin. *Frank McGuinness: Plays One* contains his early plays: *The Factory Girls, Observe the Sons of Ulster Marching Towards the Somme, Innocence, Carthaginians,* and *Baglady.* He has also translated Chekhov (*Three Sisters, Uncle Vanya*), Ibsen (*A Doll's House, Peer Gynt, Hedda Gabler*), Lorca (*Yerma*), Brecht (*The Threepenny Opera, The Caucasian Chalk Circle*) and Sophocles (*Electra*).

Alexander Ostrovsky
The Storm

a new version by
Frank McGuinness

faber and faber

First published in 1998
by Faber and Faber Limited
3 Queen Square London WC1N 3AU

Typeset by Country Setting, Kingsdown, Kent CT14 8ES
Printed in England by Intype London Ltd

A CIP record for this book
is available from the British Library

ISBN 0-571-20004-4

2 4 6 8 10 9 7 5 3 1

For Marina Carr

The Storm was first presented, in this version, by the
Almeida Theatre, London, on 12 November 1998.
The cast was was as follows:

Dikoi Sylvester Morand
Boris Richard Lynch
Kabanova Maggie Steed
Tikhon Paul Hilton
Katerina Susan Lynch
Varvara Patricia Kerrigan
Kuligin Tom Mannion
Kudryash Clarence Smith
Shapkin Nasser Gheraieb
Feklusha Maggie McCarthy
Glasha Jane Cameron
Lady Eve Pearce
Footmen Gary Cameron, Daniel Thomason

Directed by Hettie Macdonald
Designed by Robin Don
Lighting by Peter Mumford
Music by Deirdre Gribbin

Characters

Savyol Prokofyevich Dikoi
an important person around town

Boris Grigorevich
his nephew, a well-educated young man

Marfa Ignatevna Kabanova (Kabanikha)
a rich merchant's widow

Tikhon Ivanych Kabanov her son

Katerina his wife

Varvara Tikhon's sister

Kuligin
a tradesman, self-taught watchmaker,
searching for (the secret of) perpetual motion

Vanya Kudryash a young man, Dikoi's clerk

Shapkin a tradesman

Feklusha a religious pilgrim

Glasha a servant-girl at the Kabanovs'

Lady with Two Footmen
an old woman in her seventies, half-mad

Townspeople of both sexes

*The action takes place in the town of Kalinov,
on the banks of the Volga, during the summer.*

Ten days pass between Acts Three and Four.

*Author's note: all the characters, except Boris,
are dressed Russian-style.*

Act One

Two benches and a few bushes in a public park on the high bank of the Volga.
  There is a rural view beyond the Volga.
  Kuligin sits on a bench gazing across the river.
  Kudryash and Shapkin wander about.
  Kuligin sings.

Kuligin
  To stand in the soft valleys
  Where hilltops are smooth ...

  He stops singing.

A mystery, boys – I have to say it, I do – it's a mystery. Kudryash – listen, young man, I have been looking hard at the Volga every day for many long years, and do you know, I still keep on looking and looking.

Kudryash And so?

Kuligin The view – beyond belief – beautiful – so beautiful. It warms my soul.

Kudryash Is that a fact?

Kuligin The beauty of it. And 'is that a fact' – that's your response. Either you're sick seeing it or you have no – absolutely no comprehension of nature's beauty – and it is all around you.

Kudryash What point talking to you? In these parts you're an oddball – the mad professor.

Kuligin I'm self-taught – and I'm a mechanic – a mechanic.

Kudryash One and the same.

Silence.
   Kuligin points to one side.

Kuligin Look over there – who's waving their arms like a windmill, Kudryash?

Kudryash Who? Dikoi – that's who. He's tearing the lining out of his nephew.

Kuligin He's chosen a right place for it.

Kudryash He'll do it when he likes. He fears no man. Poor old Boris – his uncle's got the knife over him stretched on the altar. He has him at his mercy.

Shapkin You'd travel far to find a harder boss than the brave Dikoi. He'd rip a man to shreds for looking at him.

Kudryash The man's a peasant – a thick, loud, dirty peasant.

Shapkin Kabanova – she's as bad.

Kudryash She hides it under the cloak of holiness – that one, but him, he's a mad dog let off the chain –

Shapkin Nobody can put manners on him – that's why he'd fight with his shadow.

Kudryash If there were a few boys like myself about, we'd soon put a halt to his dirty gallop.

Shapkin Is that a fact – what would you do?

Kudryash Scare the shit out of him, once and for all.

Shapkin How?

Kudryash Four or five of us would meet him in an alley – have a tiny talk, man to man, and he would be like a woman's scarf in our fists. He would not squeak about the little lesson we have taught him. He'd just watch himself wherever he went.

Shapkin It's no wonder he wanted you posted off to the army.

Kudryash He did want to, but he didn't. So long to that notion. He won't send me away. That nose of his can smell what's in store for him if he tried that, and it's not nice. He might put the shivers up you, but me, I can talk to him.

Shapkin Can you?

Kudryash What do you mean, can you? Look, there's some consider me a hard man – so why does he keep me on? It must mean he needs me. And that means I've no fear of him – but if he's wise, he might be afraid of me – he might –

Shapkin So he hasn't a mouth like a sewer when he speaks to you?

Kudryash Jesus, of course he has. It's meat and drink to him. But I miss nothing. If he says one word to me, I say ten back to him. He spits and walks away then. There is not a chance I'd lower myself in front of him.

Kuligin Then why are you following his example? Better put up with it.

Kudryash If you're so smart why don't you put some manners into him first, and then you can start on the rest of us. It's a pity his daughters are still in their teens. None of them is ready for it yet.

Shapkin What are you talking about?

Kudryash I'd have put a smile on his face. I have a way with women.

Dikoi and Boris go past.
Kuligin takes off his cap.

Shapkin Come on – move off. Give him no chance to start on us.

Kudryash and Shapkin move off.

Dikoi Why are you sneaking about here? You're some lazy git. Go to hell.

Boris This is my day off. What have I to do in the house?

Dikoi If you wanted to, you'd find something to do. If I've told once, I've told you twice, don't dare let me set eyes on you, but there's no stopping you. Is there not enough room for you or something? No matter where I go, you're standing in front of me. Damn you, go to hell. You're standing there like the trunk of a tree – why? Damn you, I'm talking to you.

Boris And I'm listening – what else can I do?

Dikoi Clear off. I don't want to talk to you – you're jaundiced as a Jesuit.

Dikoi goes off.

You're like the worms – you're everywhere.

He spits and goes out.

Kuligin Why do you have anything to do with that man, sir? Nobody can understand it. Why do you want to live with him and endure all that abuse?

Boris Kuligin, it's not that I want to – I have to.

Kuligin If I might ask, why do you have to, sir? Tell us, sir, if you can.

Boris Why shouldn't I tell you? Didn't you know our grandmother Anfisa?

Kuligin How could anybody not know her?

Kudryash That's true.

Boris She turned against my father because he married a noble woman. That's why father and mother went to live in Moscow. Mother told me she couldn't live three days with her in-laws before things turned very rough.

Kuligin Well, it's rough for you here now, sir. That's the only word for it. You'll need to get used to it, sir.

Boris My parents reared us well in Moscow. We wanted for nothing. I was sent to the Commercial Academy and my sister to boarding school. Then the cholera took the two of them. Myself and my sister were orphans. We heard next, grandmother had passed away as well. She'd left a will instructing our uncle to pay us our share when we come of age, but with one condition.

Kuligin Which was, sir?

Boris We should show him respect.

Kuligin So you'll never see your money, sir, that's for sure.

Boris It's worse than that, Kuligin. First he'll mock us, then as the mood hits him he'll harm us in every way he can, and it will end up with us getting nothing or next to it. Even then, he'll be touring the town saying he handed it over out of his own charity, and we were not entitled to it.

Kudryash Well, that's the way with the business men in this place. And if you do show him respect, who's going to stop him saying you don't?

Boris You have it exactly. Even now you hear him saying 'I have my own youngsters. Why should I throw money at somebody else's? That way I hurt my own.'

Kuligin A dirty business as far as you're concerned, sir.

Boris It wouldn't matter if it were just me. I'd pack the whole thing in and leave. But my sister – her I feel sorry for. He wanted her sent here as well. My mother's family wouldn't allow it. They wrote she was ill. What kind of life would she lead here – I can't think about it.

Kudryash That goes without saying. They have no idea how to treat people.

Kuligin How do you live with him, sir? What's your position?

Boris None – none at all. He says, 'You can live with me, you do as you're bid to do and you take what wages I pay you.' That means in a year's time he'll work out whatever sum suits him.

Kudryash That's his way all the time. No one dare whisper against what he pays us – he'll eat the face of you. He says, 'Who are you to know what's in my mind? Can you read my soul? Maybe I might have the notion to hand five thousand over to you.' You just try and talk to him. Never once in all his days has he had such a notion.

Kuligin Well, what's to be done, sir? You'll have to try to humour him.

Boris How – that's the trouble Kuligin – there is no way it's possible. His own flesh and blood can't humour him. How can I?

14

Kudryash How can anybody? He leads his life to abuse other people. And that's really true when it's to do with money. Every bill causes an argument. People are willing to settle if that will calm him down. And don't let anybody annoy him first thing in the morning. He explodes. And he'll be on our backs the whole day.

Boris My aunt has tears in her eyes every day, begging us all, 'Don't get him angry, my dears – don't get him angry!'

Kudryash You can't stop it. If he turns up in the market, that's the end of it. He hurls insults at all the peasants. Even if they're making a loss, he won't leave until he has abused them. That's his mood for the rest of the day.

Shapkin There's a word for him – he's a bruiser.

Kudryash He is that and more.

Boris The real bother starts when someone offends him and he can't offend back. The whole house walks on tiptoes then.

Kudryash That time on the Volga ferry – a hussar called him by a fair few names – that was some laugh. That was wonderful.

Boris And everybody at home suffered for it. For two weeks after that they were hiding in attics and storerooms.

Kuligin Who's that? Are people out already from the evening service?

Several people pass by at the back of the stage.

Kudryash Shapkin, we'll go for a drink. Nothing to stand here for.

They bow and go out.

Boris It is very rough for me here, Kuligin. I'm not used to it. I get the strangest looks from everyone. It's as if I don't belong – as if I'm getting in their way. I don't know how people do things here. I know it's Russian – it's our own way, but somehow I can't get used to it.

Kuligin Sir, you never will.

Boris Why?

Kuligin Savage, sir – this town is savage. The poor have nothing but their poverty and that hammers the hardness into them. And we will never, ever change that, sir. You work like a honest man, but all you'll earn will buy your daily bread, and no more than that ever. And if some boy has money, he'll treat the poor man like a slave – one goes without wages so that the other grows richer. Do you know what your uncle said to the mayor? The peasants came to the mayor, they were complaining your uncle had not settled up fairly with a single one of them. The mayor said to him, 'Listen here, pay what you owe fair and square to the peasants.' That uncle of yours pats the mayor on the shoulder and says, 'Your excellency, why should the likes of us talk about nonsense like that? Is it worth it? In the space of one year I deal with a lot of people. Just think about this. If I hold back a kopeck or two from all of them, that way I'll make a thousand out of it, and that's the way it should be.' His words, sir. But look how the rich behave among themselves. Stabbing each other in the back – not for profit but for pettiness. That's their pleasure. They can't stand each other. They'll lure some drunken clerk to their big houses, sir. The kind of clerk who's like the living dead – the humanity's been drunk out of him. For a small fee these boyos scribble the worst slander about people's closest relations on stamped paper – official paper. The law suits start then, and so does the endless misery. They're never out of the courts here, then they go to the courts in the city. The lawyers there see them coming and they rub their hands with glee. The song's soon sung, as they say, but the business goes on and on. They lead them by the nose here, there and everywhere. They drag it out to eternity, and this whole prolonged battle makes the richies rub their hands even harder, because this is what suits them. They say, 'This might cost me a fair whack of money, but it's going to cost the other fellow his fair whack as well.' I'd like to work the whole thing into a poem.

Boris You can write poetry?

Kuligin In the old way, sir. I've read plenty of Lomonosov, Derzhavin. Lomonosov was a wise man, a true student of nature. He was one of our own, you know – he came from poor people.

Boris Do write it. It would make interesting reading.

Kuligin How sir? They'd swallow me up without salt. As things stand, sir, I get it in the neck for talking too much. I can't help that. I love a good conversation – share the talk, I say. I'll tell you something about family life in this place, sir, but maybe some other time. That makes interesting hearing as well.

Feklusha enters with another woman.

Feklusha Bunderful, my precious, bunderful. Really beautiful. I can say no more. This is the promised land, and you are living in it. Your merchants – really holy people – they are steeped in so many virtues. The generosity of them – the charity. I'm so happy, my precious, my heart is coming up my throat, it is so happy. And they'll get back what they've given – they'll get more back for helping us, especially at the Kabanovs' house.

Boris Kabanovs?

Kuligin Kabanova – the mother – a breast-beating hypocrite of the highest order. She'd give her last bite to the beggars, but she'd cut the ears of her own people.

Silence.

I'd love to discover the secret of perpetual motion, sir.

Boris What would you do with it?

Kuligin What wouldn't I do, sir? Do you know the English are offering a million to the man who finds it? I'd hand over all the money for the good of society to help people. Ordinary people need work to be given to them. As it stands, too many hands have nothing worth doing.

Boris So you're hoping to find the secret of perpetual motion?

Kuligin And I will not fail, sir. All I need now is to raise a bit of money and build a model. Goodbye, sir.

He goes out.

SCENE FOUR

Boris I don't want to disillusion him. He's a good man. He has dreams, and he is happy. Me – I'm wasting my youth in this hellhole. That much is clear. I am completely under another man's heel and now I start to entertain this nonsense. I do not need this. Why does my heart want to break? Nothing to offer – shat on – and like a fool I fall in love. Who with? A woman that I will never even talk to.

Silence.

I can't get her out of my head, no matter how hard I try. She's coming. She's with her husband, and her mother-in-law is with them. I am a fool – I am. I'll take a look from round the corner, then I'll head home.

He goes out.

SCENE FIVE

Kabanova, Kabanov, Katerina and Varvara enter from the opposite side.

Kabanova Your mother is speaking – listen to her. Do exactly what I told you to do as soon as you get there.

Kabanov Mother, I am listening – I always do what you say.

Kabanova These days there's not much respect for the old.

Varvara (*in an aside*) Not respect you – Jesus Christ.

Kabanov Mother, I think I can't make a move or a mistake without your say-so.

Kabanova I would believe that, young man, if my own eyes had not seen and my own ears had not heard what's become of the respect children have for their parents. The pain – the pain children bring to their mother – at least they might understand that.

Kabanov Mother, I –

Kabanova The woman who gave birth to you – if she says something once or twice that wounds your pride, should you not put up with it? I say you should. What do you think?

Kabanov When have I not put up with anything from you, Mother?

Kabanova Your mother's an old woman – she's foolish. You're young, and you're clever – don't make too many demands on us old fools.

Kabanov sighs in an aside.

Kabanov Sweet Jesus.

He speaks to his mother.

Mother, I would not think of doing anything like that.

Kabanova Your parents are hard on you because they love you. They keep on and on at you because they love you. They want to teach you what's right but this is not acceptable any more. Children go around complaining that their mother never stops nagging – that she drains the daylight from their eyes. God help the poor woman if she whispers a word that annoys the woman who married her son. Then the word's out that the mother of the groom is digging the grave for the blushing bride.

Kabanov Mother, no one is saying anything about you.

Kabanova To my face, no – to my face, my boy. It would be a lie to say I heard anything. But if I had, I would not break breath like this to you now, son!

She sighs.

The weight of our sins. And we sin and sin and sin. You start a simple conversation, you touch on things that touch you deeply, and you get angry. That's a sin, losing your temper. Go on, son, say what you like about me. You can't forbid people talking. What they haven't the guts to say to your face, they hiss behind your back.

Kabanov May the tongue fall out of my mouth –

Kabanova Enough, enough. Don't swear an oath – that's a sin. For many a day now you're closer to your wife than to your mother. I've seen that. You used to love me. I have not seen that love from the day and hour you married her.

Kabanov In what way do you see this, Mother?

Kabanova Every way, my son. What a mother can't see with her own two eyes, her heart can tell her. Her heart feels it. Maybe it's that wife of yours, thieving you away from me. I really don't know.

Kabanov Mother, that's just not true. What are you thinking of?

Katerina Dear mother, you mean as much to me as my own mother, and Tikhon loves you too.

Kabanova Was I asking you? No. So you keep your mouth closed. Don't you shove your way in, young woman. After all, he is my son. Don't you forget that. Why are you throwing yourself forward? Do you want people to admire you? Is it so they'll see how much you adore your husband? We're all poisoned looking at you pushing your love into people's faces.

Varvara (*in an aside*) Lovely place to lecture us all.

Katerina What you're saying about me, mother, is not just. If I am with people or I'm without them, I'm the same always. I do not make a show of myself.

Kabanova You were far from my thoughts when I was talking. The words just slipped out of me.

Katerina Whether they did or they didn't, why do you want to insult me?

Kabanova The little bird's feathers have been ruffled – the important lady is offended.

Katerina Nobody likes to be wrongly accused.

Kabanova Yes, I know you haven't got it in you to hear my words – what can I do, I'm only your mother. My heart breaks for you. I read it long ago that you two want to do just as you please. Wait a bit, when I'm under the clay you can have your own way. Do as you desire then no trouble from the old ones. And you might – might remember me.

Kabanov Mother, day and night we pray to God that God protects you, and grants you every blessing and all success in your business.

Kabanova I've heard enough – please let things be. One time perhaps you did love your mother when you were free of the marriage bed. How can you have time for me now? Your wife's young, you've got her.

Kabanov One doesn't rub out the other. My wife's my wife, but I'll always respect my mother – I shouldn't have to say it.

Kabanova So you'd swop your wife for your mother? I wouldn't believe that in this life.

Kabanov Why should I swop anything? I love the two of you –

Kabanova Shovel it on thick, yes, go on. I can see I stand in your way.

Kabanov See what you like. Suit yourself. Why was I born into this world with the misfortune that I can never please you? Can you tell me?

Kabanova Listen to the song of the little orphan boy. Why are you crying like a cissy? What kind of husband are you? Take a hard look at yourself. After this show, do you think your wife will fear you?

Kabanov Why should she fear me? She loves me, that contents me enough.

Kabanova Why should she fear you – what is this? Why should she fear what you say? Have you lost your reason – have you? If she does not fear you, then she will not fear me. She will not need to. What then will be unleashed in the house? She is your wife by law, isn't she? Does the law mean nothing to you? If you have stuffed your head with such stupidity, at least stop spouting it out in front of your sister. She's a young girl. She'll get married too. And after she's followed your example, her husband is not going to thank us for it! Look at him – not a brain in his head and he wants to lead his life his own way.

Kabanov Mother, I don't want to lead my life my own way. How could I – how?

Kabanova So you think it's all hold me tight and kiss me quick with your wife? You won't roar at her, you won't raise your fist?

Kabanov Mother, I –

She is agitated.

Kabanova She could lead on another man and turn him into her lover. And you'd let them. Yes? Say something.

Kabanov Mother, for God's sake –

She answers absolutely cold-bloodedly.

Kabanova Idiot.

She sighs.

What can I say to an idiot? It's just another sin.

Silence.

I'm going home.

Kabanov We'll be there soon. We'll just have a stroll up and down the boulevard.

Kabanova Do what you like. Just make certain I don't have to wait for you. I don't like that, as you well know.

Kabanov Mother, we won't. God forbid.

Kabanova See to it.

She goes out.

Kabanov Do you see now I have to take mother's worst word about you? The life I have!

Katerina And this in some way is *my* fault?

Kabanov Whose fault it is I don't know.

Varvara No, how would you?

Kabanov And she would once keep on at me, 'Get married. Just get married. I want to see you a married man.' Now she finds nothing right, she's always at me, and it's all because of you!

Varvara It's not her fault. Mother keeps attacking her – you do too. Then you run around saying you love your wife. I could vomit looking at you.

Kabanov What's the point of talking? What am I to do?

Varvara Know where you stand. And if you've nothing better to do, keep your mouth shut. Why are you shifting from one foot to the other? I can read you like a book, I know what you're planning.

Kabanov Which is what?

Varvara Do I need to tell you? You want off to Dikoi's house and drink with him. Yes?

Kabanov Spot on, dear sister.

Katerina Then hurry, Tisha, or your mother will start up again.

Varvara Down your drink quickly, or you know what's in store.

Kabanov As if I didn't.

Varvara We're not getting into hot water for you. We don't want to.

Kabanov Won't be a minute. Wait for me.

He goes out.

SCENE SEVEN

Katerina You feel sorry for me, Varvara, do you?

Varvara looks away.

Varvara Yes I do.

Katerina So you *do* love me?

She kisses her warmly.

Varvara Why in God's name should I not love you?

Katerina You're so kind. I'm dying about you.

Silence.

Something's just come into my head.

Varvara What?

Katerina Why can't human beings fly?

Varvara What are you saying?

Katerina What I mean is why can't we fly like birds?

I sometimes think that I am a bird. When you stand on a big height, you're tempted to fly. I'll run a bit, spread out my arms, and take to the air. Will we try it now?

She makes to run.

Varvara What in the name of God has entered your head?

Katerina sighs.

Katerina I used to be bursting with life. But at your house I've faded entirely.

Varvara Do you think I've not watched you?

Katerina The girl I used to be! I had nothing to hold me down, a bird in flight. Mama was mad about me. Dressed me up like a little doll. Didn't let me do a hand's turn of work. I could do exactly what I liked. Do you know how I lived when I was a child? I'll tell you. I'd rise early in the morning. If it was summer I'd walk down to the spring and wash myself. I'd fetch water back with me, and I'd water the flowers in the house. All of them. I had mountains and mountains of flowers. Mama and I would go to church, along with all the women on their pilgrimage. Our house was packed with pilgrims – women who believed devoutly. We'd come back and we'd sit working at something or other, threading gold through velvet, and the women would tell us where their pilgrimage had taken them, what they'd seen there and the lives of the saints, or they would sing the psalms. We passed the time to dinner like that. The old women would lie down for a sleep then. I would stroll in the garden. Then it was time for vespers and in the evening more stories, more singing. That's how wonderful it was.

Varvara We do the same here.

Katerina We do, but it's as if we're forced to. I loved going to church then, I really did. It was entering the gates of heaven, I thought. I could see nothing, remember nothing, didn't know when the service ended. It had all passed by me in an instant. Everyone was looking at me, Mama said, to see what had come over me. Do you know something? If the day was sunny a big blast of light poured down from the dome and it lit up the smoke from the incense, that was floating like clouds. And in that light there were angels flying around, they were singing. I could see them. I'd get up at night when I was a girl – I remember this and we had little lamps burning everywhere beneath the icons. I'd kneel in a corner somewhere and pray until the morning came. Maybe I'd go out into the garden early in the day as the sun was starting to show his face. I'd kneel, pray and weep. I don't know why, but that would be how they found me. What was I praying about – what was I asking for? I don't know. I needed nothing. I was content. But the dreams, Varvara, such dreams I dreamt. Temples of gold. Gardens the like you never smelt before nor ever set eyes on. And always voices you could not see were singing. And the clear perfume of the cypress. Hills and trees, they weren't like the way they usually are, but like the way they are written in icons. It was as if I could fly, I was flying through the air. I do still dream now and then, but not often, and never like that.

Varvara What do you dream now?

Katerina I'll die soon.

Varvara Stop.

Katerina No, I'm going to die. Something bad is happening to me, Varya. Something strange. Never felt this before. Something's inside me – I can't believe it. It's as if I'm coming back to life – I don't know, I don't.

Varvara What's happening to you?

She takes her by the hand.

Katerina Something bad, Varvara. I'm very afraid, I'm very afraid. It's as if I'm standing at the end of the earth and something is edging me towards it. I can do nothing to hold my ground.

Varvara What's wrong with you? Are you all right?

Katerina I am, yes. If I were sick, it would be better – this would not be so bad. Notions – I have notions – and I can't get rid of them. I try to think of something else, but they're lodged in my brain. I pray but I can't finish my prayers. My tongue takes me through the words, but they're not what's in my mind. Maybe it's the devil, spitting in my ear, telling me filthy things. The things I imagine, it makes my skin crawl thinking about them. What's wrong with me? Something terrible is going to happen. I get no sleep at night, Varvara. I hear whispering, as if someone is soothing me, and they sound like the sigh of a dove. I don't dream the way I used to of the trees and hills of heaven, Varvara. Someone seems to be grabbing hold of me, it's fierce, and he's taking me somewhere so I follow him, I follow –

Varvara And?

Katerina Why am I telling you this? You're not a married woman.

Varvara looks around.

Varvara Tell me. I dream worse than you.

Katerina How can I tell you? I'm ashamed.

Varvara No need to be. Tell me.

Katerina At home I am suffocating – suffocating – I want to run clean away. The notion hits me, if I had my way, I would be on the Volga now, in a boat there would be music. Or I could be in a beautiful troika, and all around me the fierce arms –

Varvara Of a man who is not your husband.

Katerina How could you know that?

Varvara How could I not?

Katerina Varya, the sins I've committed in my mind. I've tried to stop it, I've shed sore tears, unfortunate woman that I am. But it is a sin and I cannot stop it. I've nowhere to turn. Is it so wicked? Varvara, is it such a filthy sin that I love another man?

Varvara I don't judge you. I have my own sins.

Katerina What am I going to do? I'm weak as a child. Where will I go? If this pain lasts, I'll harm myself.

Varvara Come on now. What's wrong with you? Wait a little while. My brother's away from tomorrow. Then we can put our heads together. You might be able to see each other.

Katerina No – no need for that. Christ preserve us, what are you planning?

Varvara What are you so afraid of?

Katerina If I should ever meet this man, even once, I would turn my back on home, and nothing in this world would make me return there.

Varvara Wait a while – wait and we'll see.

Katerina No. Stop saying that. No. I don't even want to listen.

Varvara So you'll let yourself waste away into nothing? And if you die roaring with remorse, do you think anyone will shed a tear over you? Try it and find out for yourself. Why are you tormenting yourself like this?

An old lady with a walking stick enters.
Two servants in three cornered hats follow from behind.

SCENE EIGHT

Lady My beautiful girls, what is going on? What are you doing here? Are you waiting for your young men to admire you? Good times, yes? Having a good time. Does your beauty fill you up with joy? Look where beauty leads you.

She points to the Volga.

In there – right down – there to the end of the earth.

Varvara smiles.

You're smiling – what at? Forget all pleasure.

She raps with her stick.

There is an endless, eternal fire and you will all burn in it. You will all boil in the black burning tar of hideous hell. Beauty – down there, that's where it ends – down there.

She exits.

SCENE NINE

Katerina I'm shaking like a leaf. That woman terrified me. It was as if she were making some kind of prophecy about me.

Varvara Throw her curses on her own head, the old witch.

Katerina Why did she speak like that? Why did she say it?

Varvara Badness. Pay no heed to her. That's how she talks to everybody. Since she was young, she's spent her whole life sinning. Ask anyone. Things people could tell you about that one. She's going to die, she's a frightened woman, that's what's wrong there. Whatever frightens her she wants to frighten other people with. Even the young boys in the town shy away from her. She waves her stick at them and she roars, 'You're going to burn in the fire.'

Katerina tightens her eyes.

Katerina Stop. She put my heart crosswise.

Varvara What, are you afraid? That old fool?

Katerina She scared me to death. I can't get rid of the sight of her.

Silence.
Varvara looks around.

Varvara Where's my brother? I feel a thunderstorm coming.

Katerina reacts with horror.

Katerina A storm? Let's get home – now.

Varvara Have you totally taken leave of your senses? You can't go home without my brother. How could you show your face?

Katerina Home – let's go home. Don't bother about him.

Varvara Why are you so terrified? The storm is still miles away.

Katerina If that's the case we can wait a bit, but it would be better to leave. It's best we leave.

Varvara Look, if something's going to happen, hiding at home won't save you.

Katerina At home it's easier, it's calmer – I can pray to God before the icons.

Varvara I never knew you were petrified of storms. Me – I don't care.

Katerina How can you not be afraid? Everyone should be. It's not that they can kill you that terrifies me, but what if you die suddenly, just as you are, scarred by all your sins and wicked thoughts? I have no fear of dying, but to appear before God in the state I'm in now, after the conversation we've had, that does frighten me. The notions I've entertained. The sin I've committed. I daren't even mouth the words – I daren't.

Thunder.

Katerina Jesus.

Kabanov enters.

Varvara Here's my brother.

She speaks to Kabanov.

Get a move on. Hurry.

Thunder.

Katerina Quick, please. Hurry.

Act Two

A room in the Kabanov house. Glasha gathers up clothes in baskets.
Feklusha enters

Feklusha Are you still hard at it, little pet? What are you doing, my precious?

Glasha Getting the master ready for the road.

Feklusha He going away, the light of our life.

Glasha He is.

Feklusha And the sweet boy going for long?

Glasha Not long, no.

Feklusha God speed him. Will his wife be wailing for him or will she not?

Glasha Can't say.

Feklusha Does she wail the odd time?

Glasha Never heard.

Feklusha It does my heart power of good to hear a young girl giving a grand wail.

Silence.

Listen, my girl, keep a sharp eye on that beggar woman. Take care she doesn't lift something.

Glasha What is wrong with you all? You tell tales on each other. Can you not be content to live and let live? When you're with us, you pilgrims have the best of lives,

33

but you're constantly at each other's throats arguing. Aren't you afraid you're committing sin?

Feklusha Where there's life there's sin, my dear. That's the world we live in. Know what I say? Simple folk like yourself, my precious, you only fight against one devil. Our people, the pilgrims, we have between six to twelve battling us and we have to beat each and every one to pulp. Hard work, sweet girl.

Glasha Why are there so many at you?

Feklusha The devil is our enemy and he hates us because we lead such holy lives. And I, my good girl, I do not stir up bother. Not a sin of mine. I do however have one sin and I well know what it is. I love the best of food. And what about it? God indulges me in my weakness.

Glasha So you've travelled to many places, Feklusha?

Feklusha No, I haven't – because of the weakness, my sweet. But I have heard about those who have – heard plenty. Some lands haven't even a Christian tsar to their name. They have sultans to rule over them. In one land the Turkish sultan Makhsut sits on the throne, and in the other there's the Persian sultan Makhaut. They pass judgement over all the people, little pet, and all their judgements are wrong. They can get nothing fair and just because of what they believe in. With us, the law is always righteous but with them, dear, it is unrighteous. What our just law states, their law contradicts. And all the judges in these other countries, they're not just either. So, my precious, they write in their petitions 'Judge me now, you dirty judge.' There is another country where people bark like dogs.

Glasha Why?

Feklusha Because they all have dog's heads.

Glasha Why?

Feklusha Because they don't believe in God. Pagans. I'm off on a little stroll around the big houses. Maybe they'll have something for the poor. Cheerio now.

Glasha Bye.

Feklusha goes out.

The size of the world – God knows. Strange places there must be on this earth – very strange. We sit here and we know nothing. Isn't it as well that holy people can tell you the doings of the big wide world? If they didn't, we die as fools. All of us.

Katerina and Varvara enter.

SCENE TWO

Varvara Get those bundles down to the wagon, Glasha – the horses have come.

She turns to Katerina.

They made you tie the knot too young. You never had a chance to enjoy yourself when you were a girl. That's why your heart hasn't calmed itself.

Katerina And it never will calm.

Varvara Why say that?

Katerina That's the way I was born – a passionate soul. When I was only six years old – listen to this – someone upset me over something or other. Even though it was nearly night, I raced down to the Volga, I found a boat and pushed myself off from the shore. They found me the next morning miles away.

Varvara Did the lads never give you the look?

Katerina They did indeed.

Varvara And you – did you fall for anyone?

Katerina Me – I laughed.

Varvara Katerina, you don't love Tikhon, do you?

Katerina Love him – what do you mean? I'm sorry for him, truly sorry.

Varvara Then you don't love him. You can't, if you're sorry for him. And if you tell the truth, you never will. Stop hiding that from me. I noticed a while ago you love someone else.

Katerina is frightened.

Katerina How did you notice?

Varvara You're a comical character. Do you think I'm simple? The first sign – you see him and straightaway your whole face changes.

Katerina begins to lower her eyes.

Varvara That's the least of it.

Katerina So, who is it?

Varvara You know. Why should I spell it out?

Katerina Say it. His name – tell me.

Varvara Boris Grigorevich.

Katerina That's him, yes, Varya, him. Varya, for the love of God –

Varvara I would not. Just mind you don't give it away yourself.

Katerina I can't lie. I don't know how to hide it.

Varvara You must. Remember where you live. What holds this house together? Lies. Even I wasn't much of a liar, but I learned to be – I had to. Yesterday I was out walking. I saw him and talked.

There is a brief silence.
Katerina keeps her eyes lowered.

Katerina And?

Varvara Sent his regards. Said there was nowhere you can see each other. That it was a shame.

Katerina lowers her head even further.

Katerina Nowhere? Yes, what would be the point –

Varvara He looked the picture of misery.

Katerina Stop talking about him. Please say nothing. I don't want to know him. I *will* love my husband. Tisha, I will not change you for anyone, my darling. I didn't even want to think about it, but you have me all confused now.

Varvara Don't think about it. Who's making you?

Katerina Have you not an ounce of pity for me? Don't think about it, you say, when you yourself remind me? Do you believe I want to think about him? I cannot get him out of my head – what do I have to do? He's in front of my eyes no matter what I imagine. I want to get a grip on myself, but I can't. Do you know what? The devil touched my soul again last night. I nearly fled from the house.

Varvara God love you, but you are a tangled knot. I'll give you my opinion. Do what you want, but keep it all safe and sound.

Katerina Not that way – no. What good is that? Better to endure this as long as I can.

Varvara And if you can't endure it, what then?

Katerina What will I do?

Varvara Yes – what?

Katerina The first thing comes into my head – that's what.

Varvara Try it. They will devour you here.

Katerina What's that to me? I'll be out of here, and that is that.

Varvara Where? You are a married woman.

Katerina Varya, you do not know me. May God forbid this happening, but if things turn truly against me, there is no power could stop what I'd do. I'd hurl myself from the window, drown myself in the Volga. I do not want to live here and I will not, even if you tear me limb from limb.

Silence.

Varvara Katya – when Tikhon's left, we'll sleep in the garden, in the summerhouse.

Katerina Why, Varya?

Varvara Why not – it's all the same, yes?

Katerina I'd be scared to sleep in a place I didn't know.

Varvara What's there to scare you? Glasha will be with us.

Katerina It still makes me a bit nervous. All right, yes.

Varvara I wouldn't have asked you, but I needed to. Mama won't let me do it on my own.

Katerina looks at her.

Katerina Why do you need to?

Varvara laughs.

Varvara We can tell each other what the future holds in store.

Katerina You're joking, aren't you?

Varvara Of course I am – what did you think?

Silence

Katerina Where's Tikhon got to?

Varvara Why do you need him?

Katerina Just wondering. He's leaving soon.

Varvara Locked himself away with mother. She's gnawing away at him, like rust into iron.

Katerina For what reason?

Varvara No particular reason, just giving him his code of conduct. He'll be travelling – out of her sight for two weeks. She's tearing her heart out that he's slipped her chains. Just now she'll be listing out her instructions, each one more demanding than the last. Then she'll march him up to the icon – she'll make him swear he'll follow her words of warning to the letter.

Katerina So even when he has slipped the chains, he's tied hand and foot to her still?

Varvara Tied – what do you mean? As soon as he hits the road, he hits the bottle. He's listening now, thinking only how quickly he can disappear.

Kabanova and Kabanov enter.

Kabanova Now you remember everything I've told you. Do you hear? Make sure you do – I hope something has stuck in your thick skull.

Kabanov Mother, I'll remember.

Kabanova So, everything's ready. The horses are here. Make your goodbyes and God be with you.

Kabanov Yes, mother, it's time.

Kabanova So?

Kabanov Is there something you want?

Kabanova You're standing there, do you not know what has to be done? Order your wife what to do when you're not here.

Katerina drops her eyes to the ground.

Kabanov She knows herself.

Kabanova Don't start arguing. Order her. And let me hear what you're instructing her. Then when you come back, you can ask her if she's done it all.

He stands in front of Katerina.

Kabanov If mother tells you to do something, Katya, do it.

Kabanova Show no bad manners to her mother-in-law – tell her.

Kabanov No bad manners.

Kabanova Respect her mother-in-law like her own mother – she should do that.

Kabanov Respect Mama like your own mother, Katya.

Kabanova Sitting about with nothing to do, like some fancy lady, she should not do that.

Kabanov Do some work while I'm away.

Kabanova And stop her staring out the windows.

Kabanov Mother, when would she –

Kabanova Tell her.

Kabanov Don't stare out the window.

Kabanova And she should not stare at young men when you're away.

Kabanov For God's sake, really, Mama –

She answers severely.

Kabanova Stop beating about the bush and do what your mother tells you.

She adds with a smile.

Everything is safer when you spell it out.

He is embarrassed.

Kabanov Don't stare at young men.

Katerina gives him a severe look.

Kabanova Right, if you need them, you can have a few words together now. Varvara, come with me.

They exit.
Katerina stands in a state of numbness.

SCENE FOUR

Kabanov Katya?

Silence.

You're not angry with me, Katya, are you?

After a short silence she shakes her head.

Katerina No.

Kabanov Then why are you like this? Please forgive me.

Katerina All right. It's her. She hurt me.

Kabanov Don't take everything to heart or it will destroy you. Never listen to her. She always has to say her piece. Let it go in one ear and out the other. So, I'll see you, Katya.

She flings her arms around his neck.

Katerina Don't leave, Tisha. Don't leave, please. I'm begging you, darling.

Kabanov No, Katya. My mother's sending me, how can I not go?

Katerina Take me – take me with you.

He frees himself from her embrace.

Kabanov I can't.

Katerina Why not?

Kabanov I wouldn't enjoy myself with you. I'm worn out here by women. I can't wait to be away, yet you're hanging round my neck.

Katerina You don't love me any more then?

Kabanov It's not that. But to free myself from this sentence I'd leave any wife, no matter what she looked like. I may not amount to much, but I'm still a man. If you had my life, *you'd* want to run away from your wife. For the next two weeks I know there's no threat hanging over my head, no chains tied round me, so why should I think about my wife?

42

Katerina How can I love you when you say words like that?

Kabanov They're only words. What more should I say? You're hardly on your own, you know. You're staying with my mother.

Katerina Don't speak of her – don't break my heart. Jesus, the pain.

She weeps.

What is this unfortunate woman to do? Who will protect me? Saints in Heaven, look down on me.

Kabanov Enough.

She clings to him.

Katerina Tisha, if you'd just stay or else take me with you. I would really love you, you would be all that mattered to me, darling.

She caresses him.

Kabanov Katya, I don't understand you. One minute you won't talk to me, let alone touch me. The next you're throwing yourself at me.

Katerina Tisha, why are you leaving me? Without you here, there's going to be trouble. There will be.

Kabanov If there is, what can I do?

Katerina You can do this. Make me swear a vow to you –

Kabanov Vow?

Katerina I must not meet or speak to any man when you're away. I must not think of anyone but you.

Kabanov In God's name why?

Katerina As an act of kindness to me – please.

Kabanov How can you swear something like that? Hearing this a man could think anything.

She falls to her knees.

Katerina May I never set eyes on my father and mother again. May I die with sin on my soul if I –

He brings her to her feet.

Kabanov Stop saying that – stop – it's a sin. I don't want to hear talk like that.

Kabanova's voice calls off stage. 'Time to leave, Tikhon.'
Kabanova, Varvara and Glasha enter.

SCENE FIVE

Kabanova Come on, time to leave. God go with you.

She sits down.

Kabanova Sit.

Silence.
They all sit.

Right. Goodbye.

She rises and so do the others.
He goes up to his mother.

Kabanov Goodbye, mother.

She points to the ground.

Kabanova Bow – come on bow.

He makes a low bow to the ground and kisses his mother.

Say goodbye to your wife.

Kabanov Katya, goodbye.

She throws herself on his neck.

Kabanova What do you think you are doing – have you no shame, throwing yourself on him? You're not saying goodbye to your sweetheart. He's your husband. The man of the house. Do you not know how things are done? Bow.

Katerina makes a low bow to Kabanov.

Kabanov Goodbye, sister dear.

He kisses Varvara.

Glasha, goodbye. Goodbye Mother.

He bows.

Kabanova Goodbye. Go, before there's more tears.

He goes, followed by Katerina, Varvara and Glasha.

SCENE SIX

Kabanova is alone.

Kabanova Young people – what can you do with them? Looking at them would make you laugh. If they weren't my own, I'd laugh myself sick. They know nothing. They have no idea how to do things. Don't know how to see people off on a journey. It's just as well there's the old ones at home. We can keep the house together while we're still on our feet. And they're fools – they want their own way. When they get it, they make such a show of themselves, good people mock them. Some might take pity, but most just mock. They invite their guests and don't know where to seat them in proper order – they even forget one of their own relations. It's a joke – a joke. That's how the old way of things dies out. You don't want to go into other people's houses. If you set foot inside, spit and clear straight out. I really don't know what will happen when we old ones die out. How will the world not collapse? Fortunately I won't see it.

Katerina and Varvara enter.

SCENE SEVEN

Kabanova Look at you – showing off how much you loved your husband. Now I see what you mean by love. A good wife saying goodbye to her husband would have laid herself on the porch and roared for an hour and a half. Not you though – that's clear for all to see.

Katerina What's the point? I don't know how to anyway. People would laugh at me.

Kabanova There's no great skill to it. And if you loved him, you'd learn. If you don't know how to do it properly, you could have made a fist of it. But that's all words as far as you're concerned. I'm going to say my prayers to God. Don't disturb me.

Varvara I'm going out.

Kabanova speaks warmly.

Kabanova You do that. Off you go. Be happy while you have time. You'll marry and sit inside for long enough.

Katerina is left alone and pensive.

Katerina The silence in this house is everywhere. The emptiness. If we had children – if anybody had children. I have none but my own pain. I would sit with them and we'd laugh. I really love talking with children. They're angels.

Silence

If I had died when I was a child, it would have been for the best. I'd look down from the sky onto the earth, and take pleasure in things. Or I'd be invisible, I'd fly wherever I wanted. I'd fly out to the field and I would wander on the breeze from one cornflower to another like a butterfly.

She thinks for a moment.

I know what I'll do. I'll work the way I promised to, I'll go to the market and buy some linen. I'll sew underwear and give it to the poor. They'll pray for me to God. I'll sit and sew with Varvara. We won't notice the time passing. Then Tisha will be home again.

Varvara enters.

Varvara puts a scarf on her head in front of a mirror.

Varvara I'm going out for a walk. Mother's allowed Glasha to make up beds for us in the garden. There's a little gate beyond the raspberry bushes. Mother has it locked, she hides the key. I've got my hands on it and put another in its place. She'll notice nothing. Take it – you might need it.

She hands her the key.

If I see him, I'll tell him to come to the gate.

Alarmed, Katerina pushes the key away.

Katerina What for? What for? I don't need it. I don't want it.

Varvara You don't need it, but I might. Take it – it's not going to eat you.

Katerina God almighty, why are you tempting me – what's got into you? Have you lost your mind? How can you? What's got into you?

Varvara I'm not going into it. I haven't the time. I'm going for my walk.

She exits.

SCENE TEN

Katerina is alone, holding the key in her hand.

Katerina Why is she doing this? What's got into her? Off her head – she is gone off her head. And here is my way to hell. Here it is. Throw it away, far away, into the river where it will never be found. It's like a hot coal burning my hands.

She thinks for a moment.

This is how women are damned. Who could bear to be locked up like this? All sorts of notions come into your head. If they get the chance, some would be delighted to charge head-first into something. How can they do it without working it all through? It's a tall height to fall from. They will weep their life away. They will torture themselves. And the prison they're in will close tighter.

And I am in prison – in pain. Who would not weep?
And women weep sorest. What am I now? I live. I suffer.
I have no hope for myself. None. And I know I never
will. Time will make it worse. And now I commit this
sin.

She is lost in thought.

My husband's mother. She's broken me. Because of her
this house has become hateful. The very walls sicken my
stomach.

She looks thoughtfully at the key.

Throw it away? I must of course. How did it fall into
my hands? To tempt me. To ruin me.

She listens.

Someone's coming. It made my heart leap.

She hides the key in her pocket.

No – nobody. Why did I get so scared? Why did I hide
the key? Let it stay where it is. That's what fate decrees.
What sin is it to look at him, if only from a distance?
Even if I were to speak, no harm in that. But all the
same, my husband – my promise – although he himself
didn't ask it. And I might never again be given such a
chance in my whole life. Then you'll feel sorry for
yourself. You could have tried but you didn't. What's
all this I'm saying? Why am I trying to lie to myself?
I would die so long as I might see him. Why am I
pretending? Throw the key away? Not for the whole
world – no. It is mine. Come what may, I will see Boris.
Let the night come, let the night fall.

Act Three

A street.
The gates of the Kabanovs' house and in front of them a bench.
Kabanova and Feklusha sit on the bench.

Feklusha End of the world, Marfa Ignatevna, the end of the world – all the signs point to it. Your town is peaceful and quiet, but other places are Sodom itself. Noise, scrambling about, nobody ever sitting down. People running always on the move – one here, another there.

Kabanova No need to rush here. We live without hurry, my dear.

Feklusha No, why your town is so quiet is because the good people here are so virtuous, they smell like roses. Someone like yourself for instance. That's why there's calm here and such good order. What does all this hullabaloo mean? People are full of themselves. Even in Moscow people tripping over each other and they don't know why. They are all full of themselves. So they're all charging about. They imagine they're on business. There he goes, a poor fool dashing about, taking notice of nobody, thinking he's obeying some order, he gets to where he's going, the place is bare. Not a soul. 'Twas all a dream. Then he's not well, he's depressed. Another one fancies to himself he's catching up on some friend or other. Anybody else looking in from the side can see straightaway – nobody there. It's just because he's full of himself he thinks he's meeting someone. You know, when you're full of yourself you're living in a kind of a fog. In this town, on a fine evening, very few venture out of their gate and take their rest. But in Moscow the world and his wife are all out strolling and enjoying himself. And the noise is like canon fire through the streets – the noise never stop. And what is more, Marfa Ignatevna, they've harnessed up one of those dragons that breathes fire so that people can rush even more to where they're going.

Kabanova Trains – I've heard, my dear.

Feklusha I've seen it – with my own two eyes. Them that are full of themselves, they see nothing, they call it an engine, that's what it seem like, but I've seen how it prowl along on its paws like this –

She spreads out her fingers.

And the loud noise it make, even good living people can hear it.

Kabanova Call it whatever you like – an engine if you want to. People are stupid and will believe anything. But I won't set foot on it, not if you were to pour gold over me.

Feklusha May it never come to that – God save you from such a disaster. There's something else, Marfa Ignatevna, a vision I saw in Moscow. Early in the morning just as the dawn breaking, I'm walking and I see on top of a big, high house something standing on the roof with a black face. I don't need to repeat who. He was doing something with his hand like scattering something. But he wasn't. And then I worked it out. He was sowing the seeds of wickedness. In daylight they blow over all the people who are full of themselves and don't notice. That's why they're always on the move. That's why their women are skin and bone. Their bodies don't grow fat at all. It's as if they've lost something and they're looking for it with such misery in their face. I even pity them.

Kabanova That's possible, my dear. Nothing shocks me the times we live in.

Feklusha Hard times Marfa Ignatevna, hard times. And time itself – it's starting to get shorter.

Kabanova Getting shorter – what do you mean, my dear?

Feklusha Nobody notice it – how could we when we're full of ourselves? But very smart people *notice* that time's begun to get short for us. Time was summer and winter lasted and lasted, we couldn't wait till they finished, but now you blink and they're gone by you. The days and the hours of course, they've stayed the same as ever, but time is getting shorter and shorter because we're all sinners. That's what the smart people are saying.

Kabanova The world'll grow worse than that.

Feklusha As long as we don't live to see it.

Kabanova We may do, we may well do.

Dikoi enters.

Well, my good man, what are you doing outdoors so late?

Dikoi Is there anyone going to stop me?

Kabanova Why would they want to stop you?

Dikoi So there's nothing to be said about it. What do you think I am? Under orders from somebody else? Go to hell with chat like that.

Kabanova Don't roar at me. Clear off and find a lesser woman. I'm too good for your likes. Go to wherever you're going. Feklusha, we'll move inside.

Dikoi Wait, woman, hold your ground. Don't be angry. You'll be home soon enough. Your house isn't far – there it is.

Kabanov If you're here on business, don't shout. Talk like a sensible man.

Dikoi Forget business. I'm drunk that's all.

Kabanov What do you want me to do – clap you on the back?

Dikoi Neither clap nor criticise. I'm just drunk – that's the end of it. Until I sleep it off, I can do nothing to put it right.

Kabanova Away you go to sleep then.

Dikoi Where will I go?

Kabanova Home – where else?

Dikoi If I don't want to go home?

Kabanov May I ask why you shouldn't?

Dikoi My house is like a battleground.

Kabanova Who might you be battling against? You're the only warrior in there.

Dikoi And what if I am a warrior? What of it?

Kabanova What? Nothing. But spending your whole life fighting women, that doesn't say much for you as a man.

Dikoi They should do as I tell them. Or maybe you'd want me to be the one that obeys them.

Kabanova Well, you surprise me. A whole houseful at home, and they can't please the one of you.

Dikoi That's the case.

Kabanova So what do you want from me?

Dikoi Sit down and have a good yarn with me. That way my temper leaves. You're the only one in the whole town who knows how to talk with me.

Kabanova Feklusha, go and order them to make us something to eat.

Feklusha goes out.

We'll go inside.

Dikoi No, I don't want to go in – too many women.

Kabanova What's made you this angry?

Dikoi It's been like this from the first breath this morning.

Kabanova They must have asked you for money.

Dikoi It's as though the devils have agreed between themselves. First one, then another, all day long, on at me.

Kabanova They must have wanted it very badly to persist.

Dikoi I can understand – I can. But what can I do with a heart like mine? Tell me that. I do know I should fork out the money but I can't, it's against my will. You're a friend of mine, I'd feel obliged to hand money over to you should you come looking for it, but I'd curse you for asking. I'd hand it over, I would for sure, but I'd curse you. Mention money to me and my soul starts to burn, yes burn me from the inside out. At times like that I'll curse a man over nothing.

Kabanova You have no one older in your house – that's why you're the bully you are.

Dikoi No, neighbour, hold your tongue. Listen – this is the kind of thing happening to me. When I was fasting for confession during Lent, the devil ups and sends me a scrawny looking peasant. He came wanting money for carting wood. And I was tempted to sin. I did sin. I cursed him. I gave him the worst word in my stomach.

54

I nearly beat the lining out of him. There you see, that's my temper for you. After that I asked his forgiveness. I bowed down low, just like this. I'm telling you this truly. I bowed down in front of that peasant. That's where my temper lands me. Right there in the yard I bowed down in the muck to him. I bowed in front of everyone.

Kabanova Why do you deliberately work yourself up to such a state? It's not nice, neighbour.

Dikoi Deliberately?

Kabanova I know – I've seen it. The minute you see someone wanting something from you, you turn, turn your temper against your nearest and dearest. You know when you're like that no one dare approach you in a rage. That's the way it is.

Dikoi So what if it is? Who doesn't want to hold on to what's his?

Glasha enters.

Glasha Marfa Ignatevna, supper's on the table, if you please.

Kabanova Neighbour, we'll go in – come on. Take a bite of what God's given to us.

Dikoi Right you be.

Kabanova Please – this way.

She lets Dikoi go in front of her.
Glasha stands by the gate, her arms folded.

Glasha That looks like Boris Grigorevich coming. I wonder has he come for his uncle? Maybe he's taking a stroll. Yes, must be.

Boris Is my uncle with you?

Glasha He is. Do you want him or something?

Boris I've been sent to find out where he is. If he's with you, leave him there. Who needs him? Back home they're happy that he's taken himself off.

Glasha If our mistress were to marry him, she'd soon put a stop to his gallop. What am I doing – talking like a fool to you. Goodbye.

She goes out.

Boris God above, if I could just catch one glimpse of her. I can't go into the house. Nobody enters there without an invitation. The life we lead – we live in one and the same town, practically in the next house to each other and one sees the other once a week, either in church or in the street and that's that. No sooner is a girl married here than they've buried her. It's all the same.

Silence.

It would be better if I didn't see her at all. It tears my heart open – seeing her in snatches, always surrounded by people, a hundred eyes examining you. I cannot endure it. I go out for a walk and where do I always end up – here at these gates. Why do I come here? I can never see her. What's more it will cause gossip. She'll get into trouble. This is the town I've landed in.

He moves off as Kuligin moves towards him.

Kuligin Hello there, sir, are you taking a stroll?

Boris I am – having a stroll – the weather's great at the minute.

Kuligin It's great to take a stroll just now, sir. It's quiet. The air is excellent. The smell of flowers from the meadows across the Volga. A clear sky.

'An abyss has opened, full of stars,
The stars without number,
The abyss without end.'

Let's walk out on to the boulevard, sir. There's not a being about there.

Boris We will, yes.

Kuligin What is this town like, sir? They make a boulevard and it's deserted, except on holidays. Even then, they're not out for a walk – they want to show off their clothes, that's all. The only one you'll ever meet is a drunken clerk staggering home from the pub. The poor don't have the time to stroll about – they're working, morning, noon and night. If they get three hours sleep, they're lucky. What do the rich do? Wouldn't you imagine they'd want to be out, enjoying the fresh air? Not a chance. Their gates have been long locked and their dogs are off the leads. You'd think they were looking after their business or on their knees before God. But no. They haven't locked their gates for fear of robbers. They do it so no one can witness how they make their servants' lives miserable and how they tyrannise their family. What tears are wept behind these locked gates? Never seen, never heard? Behind those closed doors, sir, there is some debauchery and drunkenness. All done on the quiet. No one sees or knows anything. God above sees it. They say, you can look at me in company or out on the street but have no business with my family. I have my locks and bolts for that they say, and my dogs bite. My family life is private, they say it's secret. And we know what those secrets are. Secrets like that, sir, make one man happy and the rest – they can howl like the wolf. What are these secrets? We all know. Robbing orphans, their own flesh and blood, their nephews. Beating their servants so they won't breathe a word about what he does there. They daren't squeal. That's your secrets for you. Well, the devil take them. Do you know, sir, who does go out strolling? Young men and women. They'll thieve a little hour from their sleep so they can walk together. Here's a couple now.

Kudryash and Varvara appear. They kiss.

Boris They're kissing.

Kuligin We don't mind that here.

Kudryash leaves.
    Varvara goes up to the gates and signals to Boris to join her. He goes to her.

I'm going out onto the boulevard, sir. I won't get in your way. I'll wait there for you.

Boris All right – I'll be there soon.

Kuligin exits.
    Varvara covers her face with her headscarf.

Varvara Do you know the ravine behind the Kabanovs' garden?

Boris Yes.

Varvara Be there later tonight.

Boris Why?

Varvara Are you thick? Just be there, you'll see why then. Hurry up, he's waiting for you.

Boris exits.

He didn't know who I was. Let him work that out. And I know, tonight Katerina won't be able to help herself. She'll rush into his arms.

She goes out through the gate.

Night.
    *A ravine, covered with bushes. At the top the
Kabanovs' garden fence and a wicket gate. A path leads
down from it.*
    Kudryash enters with a guitar.

Kudryash Not a soul here. Where is she? I'll sit and
wait. Sing a song to pass the time –

    He sings.

A Cossack led his horse to water,
A dashing blade, a fierce young man.
He hears the river's lonely whisper,
Kill your wife, you know you can.
The sweet wife bows before her husband,
And she implores on bended knee,
My love, my friend, don't raise your hand.
Till evening comes, do not kill me.
Let me watch my children sleeping,
Our babes, our bairns, that I leave weeping.

    Boris enters.
    Kudryash stops singing.

Kudryash Look who's here. The meek little lamb, but
he's on the prowl as well.

Boris Kudryash, is that you?

Kudryash Yes, Boris Grigorevich, it's me –

Boris Why are you here?

Kudryash Me? I must need to be, or I'd hardly be here.
I wouldn't have come if I didn't need to. Where is God
leading you?

Boris looks around.

Boris Kudryash – look, I need to wait here. You can go somewhere else. It makes no difference to you.

Kudryash You're here for the first time aren't you? This has been my territory for quite a while. This is where I tread my path. I like you, I'd oblige you in every way, but don't challenge me, sir, on this path at night, or God help us, you'll be in harm's way. Let's have agreement rather than anger.

Boris Vanya, what's got into you?

Kudryash Vanya – why Vanya? All right, it is my name, but just get yourself off and that's that. Find a woman of your own. Enjoy yourself and it's nobody's business but your own. Don't lay a finger on anybody else's. People don't do things like that here. If they did, the boys would break their legs. And if it were my girl – well I don't know what I'd do. I'd rip the throat out of his head.

Boris Stop wasting your breath getting angry. I have no intention of robbing your girl. I wouldn't be here if I hadn't been told to.

Kudryash Who told you?

Boris I couldn't make out who – some girl or other stopped me in the street. It was dark. She said I must come here to the back of the Kabanovs' garden, where the path is.

Kudryash Who could she have been?

Boris Kudryash, can I talk straight to you – you won't spread it around?

Kudryash Speak out – fear nothing. I give you my honest word.

Boris I know nothing about this place, how you do things, your ways of living, but the hard fact is –

Kudryash You've fallen in love, yes?

Boris Yes, Kudryash.

Kudryash Then no worries. We're easy about things like that here. Girls go and do what they like, it's none of their parents' business. Only the married women sit caged at home.

Boris That's my trouble exactly.

Kudryash You surely haven't fallen for a married woman?

Boris Married – yes, Kudryash.

Kudryash Stop, give her up.

Boris Easy to say – give her up. It's all the same to you maybe – you can give up and find another. But I can't. Once I fall in love –

Kudryash Then that means you want to destroy this woman completely.

Boris God help us – God help me – no, Kudryash. How could I? Do I want to ruin her? I only want to see her somewhere. I need no more than that.

Kudryash But can you control yourself, sir? You do know what people around here are like. You know that yourself. They will devour her till the last nail is hammered into her coffin.

Boris Kudryash, please stop talking like that – you're terrifying me.

Kudryash Does she love you?

Boris I don't know.

Kudryash You've met her sometimes, have you?

Boris Once I've been to her house – with uncle. I do see her in church, and on the boulevard. How she prays,

Kudryash – if you could see her. Her lips have the smile of an angel, it's as if her whole face shines –

Kudryash Then it has to be Kabanov's young wife.

Boris It is, Kudryash.

Kudryash If that's how it is, I congratulate you.

Boris What for?

Kudryash Come on, man. If she's told you to come here, then things are advancing very nicely.

Boris So she it was who told me to come?

Kudryash Who else?

Boris No, you're mocking me – it can't be.

He clasps his hand.

Kudryash What's wrong with you?

Boris I'll go mad with joy.

Kudryash Great reason to go mad with joy that is. You just take care that you don't land yourself in serious bother and that you don't get her in trouble. Her husband may be a fool but her mother-in-law is fierce – she's an animal.

Varvara enters through the wicket gate and sings.

SCENE THREE

Varvara
 Beyond the river,
 The flowing river,
 My Vanya walks,
 My darling Vanya –

Kudryash And he buys gifts.

He whistles.
Varvara comes down the path, having hidden her
face in her handkerchief. She goes up to Boris.

Varvara Listen, man, hold your horses. It might be
worth waiting for.

She turns to Kudryash.

We'll walk by the Volga.

Kudryash Why have you taken so long? Made me wait
like this for you. I don't like that, you know.

She puts one arm around him and they go out.

Boris Am I having some kind of dream? This night, the
songs, these meetings. Men and women walking arm in
arm. This is all so new to me – and it's good, it makes
me happy. Here I am waiting for something. What is it –
I can't think – can't imagine. But my heart is on heat –
every vein is burning. What will I say to her – I don't
know, it takes away my breath, my knees are knuckling
beneath me. My heart is a fool. Once it starts burning
nothing will calm it down. Someone's coming.

Katerina quietly comes down the path, her face
hidden in a large white shawl, her eyes cast down to
the ground.
Silence.

Boris Is that you, Katerina?

Silence

How can I thank you – I don't know.

Silence.

Katerina, how much I love you, if you only knew.

He tries to take her hand.

Katerina Don't – no – don't touch me.

She is frightened but she does not raise her eyes.

Boris Don't be angry.

Katerina Get away from me, far away, you're accursed. You must know I will never be able to wash that sin away, never ever wash it away. It will weigh on my soul like a stone, a stone.

Boris Don't chase me away.

Katerina Why have you come here? Why have you come to ruin me? I'm *married*. My husband and myself must live together till the coffin lid is over us.

Boris You yourself told me to come home –

Katerina You don't understand me. You are my enemy till the coffin lid is over us.

Boris It would have been better if I had never set eyes on you.

Katerina is agitated.

Katerina What am I bringing down on myself? Where can I run from it?

Boris Calm down.

He takes her by the arm.

Boris Sit down.

Katerina Why do you want to ruin me?

Boris How in God's name could I want to ruin you when I love you more than anything in the world – more than my own self?

Katerina No – you've ruined me – no.

Boris Katerina, do you really think I am an evil man?

She shakes her head.

Katerina You've ruined me, ruined – ruined me.

Boris I swear to God I would rather die myself.

Katerina But if I leave the house at night to come to you, how could you not ruin me?

Boris You did this of your own free will.

Katerina I have no free will. If I did, I would not have come to you.

She raises her eyes and looks at Boris.
  There is a brief silence.

Your will has power over mine – don't you see that?

She flings herself on his neck. He embraces her.

Boris Thank God to be alive.

Katerina Do you know I would like to die now – now?

Boris Die? When it's good to be alive?

Katerina Living is not for me. No. I know that already.

Boris Don't please – don't say that – don't make me mourn.

Katerina It's all right, you're free like a Cossack, but me –

Boris Nobody will ever know anything about our love. Don't you know that for your sake I'll take great care.

Katerina What? Why should you care about me? No one is to blame – this is my own doing. Feel no sorrow – go ahead and ruin me. Let everybody know, let everybody see what it is I'm doing.

She embraces Boris.

If I don't fear this sin for myself, why should I fear them passing judgement. They say that it's better when you suffer for some sin on this earth.

Boris Why think about this now? We are happy.

Katerina Yes, we are. I will have my fill of time to think on that and cry my eyes out later on.

Boris I was so frightened. I thought you would chase me away.

She is smiling.

Katerina Chase you? How? Don't you hear my heart? If you hadn't come to me then I myself would have gone to you!

Boris I had no notion that you loved me.

Katerina For a long time I've loved you. You've come to us to make me sin. I saw you and I was no longer my own woman. From the first instant you had only to nod at me and I would have followed you. Had you gone to the ends of the earth, I would be behind you and I would not have looked back.

Boris Is your husband away for long?

Katerina Two weeks.

Boris A good bit of time – we can see plenty of each other.

Katerina We can, yes. And then –

She is lost in thought.

Katerina If they cage me away, then I'll die. If they don't, I'll find my way to you.

Kudryash and Varvara enter.

Varvara Well, have the two of you agreed?

Katerina hides her face in Boris's chest.

Boris We've agreed.

Varvara Go for a walk, we'll wait. Vanya will give you a shout when you need to leave.

Boris and Katerina exit.
Varvara and Kudryash sit on the bench.

Kudryash That was a good one, sneaking out by the garden gate. Very handy indeed.

Varvara All my own idea.

Kudryash You're the girl for that. That mother of yours won't catch on –

Varvara No – no. How could she? It would not enter her head.

Kudryash But what if it did –

Varvara When her head hits the pillow, she's in a deep sleep. It's in the morning she sleeps lightly.

Kudryash How can you know that? What if the devil wakes her?

Varvara What of it? Our gate, the one from the yard, is locked outside from the garden. She'll knock and she'll knock, then she'll go away. We'll say in the morning that we were sleeping so soundly we couldn't hear her. And Glasha is keeping her eyes open. If there's anything up, she'll call us. You always have to take precautions. You really have. You have to watch your step, or you're in deep water.

Kudryash strums a few chords on the guitar.
Varvara lays her head on his shoulder, as he, not
paying any attention, plays softly.
Varvara yawns.

Varvara What's the time, I wonder.

Kudryash After twelve.

Varvara How do you know?

Kudryash The night-watchman is banging the hour on
his plate.

Varvara yawns.

Varvara Time to leave. Give them a shout. Tomorrow
we'll be out earlier, so we'll have more time together.

Kudryash whistles and begins to sing loudly.

Kudryash
Everybody home, everybody home,
But I do not want to go home.

Off stage, Boris calls.

Boris I hear you.

Varvara gets up.

Varvara Goodnight then.

*She yawns and gives him a cool kiss, as though they
have long been acquainted.*

Till tomorrow. Come a bit earlier.

*She looks over to where Boris and Katerina have gone
out.*

Enough goodbyes – you're not disappearing from each
other. You'll meet tomorrow.

Katerina comes running in, followed by Boris.

Katerina Come on, we'll go, we'll go.

They go up the path.
Katerina looks back.

Goodbye.

Boris Till tomorrow.

Katerina Yes, tomorrow. Tell me what you see in your dreams.

Boris Without fail.

Kudryash sings and accompanies himself on guitar.

Kudryash
Have fun, young girl, while you've time
Till evening turns into dawn,
And love for reason, for rhyme
Till evening turns into dawn.

Varvara is at the wicket gate.

Varvara
I am a young girl who has time,
Till evening turns into dawn,
I'll love you for reason, for rhyme,
Till evening turns into dawn.

She goes out.

Kudryash
The dawn has chased off the moon,
I'll wend my way to my home.

Act Four

In the foreground a narrow, vaulted gallery of an ancient building which is beginning to decay.
   Tufts of grass and bushes in places.
   Beyond the arches the banks of the river and a view across the Volga.
   A few men and women stroll about behind the arches.

Glasha That's drizzle that is. Could there be a storm brewing?

Townsperson I'd say so.

Glasha Just as well there's somewhere to shelter.

   They all walk in under the arches.

Shapkin Loads of people out walking on the boulevard. It's a holiday and they've all turned out. The merchants' wives have dolled themselves up.

Glasha They'll find somewhere to shelter.

Townsperson They'll pack in here soon, just watch.

   Glasha examines the well.

Glasha You do know that once upon a time these walls were all decorated. You can still make it out in places.

Townsperson It was indeed. It stands to reason the walls would be decorated. Abandoned now though, overgrown, left to rack and ruin. After the fire they didn't fix things.

Glasha So, what do you think was painted here? It's quite hard to make out.

Townsperson The fires of hell.

Glasha That's right. It is.

Townsperson And there's people from every station in life going there.

Glasha I can see that, yes.

Townsperson And from every class.

Glasha Black men as well?

Townsperson Even them, yes.

Glasha What's this?

Townsperson The Lithuanian devastation. Some battle – our men fighting the Lithuanians.

Glasha What is this Lithuania then?

Townsperson Lithuania is, well, Lithuania.

Glasha They say that the Lithuanians fell down from the sky on us.

Townsperson I can't tell you that. If it was down from the sky, then so it was.

Shapkin No need to argue. Everyone knows it was from the sky. And where there was some kind of battle with them, there's burial mounds a mile high in their memory.

Glasha Anyway, that's exactly how it was.

Dikoi enters, Kuligin behind him, without his hat. They all bow and adopt a respectful pose.

SCENE TWO

Dikoi Damn it, I'm soaked to the skin.

He turns on Kuligin.

Get out of my sight. Clear off. Idiot of a man.

Kuligin But your honour, it would benefit the whole community.

Dikoi Clear off. What benefit? Who needs this benefit?

Kuligin You yourself, your honour. You could site it here, sir, on a clear spot in the boulevard. And there'd be no expense. Very little expense.

He indicates the size of every item with his hands.

A small stone column with a little bronze plate curved like this and a style, a straight little style like this, simplicity itself. I can put it all together, I can engrave the figures all by myself. Then your honour, when you or anybody else walking here wants to take a stroll you can go up and read the time. It's a beautiful spot, there's the view and everything, but it's empty. And your honour, you know yourself, we have people passing through this town who come to look at the view – it would be a feature, very distinctive – something easy on the eye.

Dikoi Why do you keep bothering my head with this balderdash? Maybe I don't want to break breath to you? You should find out whether or not I am in the mood to listen to you. Do you fancy you're my equal, do you? He's got a right bee in his bonnet about this business, damn it. So he barges in with his long snout and starts up a conversation.

Kuligin If I did come on my own business, then I'd be in the wrong. But your honour, it's for the benefit of the whole community. For the community what's ten roubles or so? There would be no need for more, sir.

Dikoi Maybe you're out to pocket it, who's to know?

Kuligin I'm offering my labour for nothing – how can I be stealing, your honour? Everybody here knows me after all! No one has a bad word to say against me.

Dikoi Well then, they can know you, I don't want to.

Kuligin Why should you wish to insult an honest man, sir?

Dikoi Why should I give you a detailed description of myself? I don't explain myself to anyone, not even to much more important men than you. To others, you might be an honest man but me, I think you're a thief and that's that. So do you want to go to the court about it? Then know this – you are a worm. I'll show mercy if I want to. But if I don't, I will squash you.

Kuligin God be good to you, sir. Your honour, I'm a small man who's easy to insult. But I put this to you, 'Respect virtue, even if it's in rags.'

Dikoi Don't dare show me such bad manners. Do you hear?

Kuligin I'm not being bad mannered. I say this to you because you may one day take it into your head to do something for the town. You have your fair share of power, your honour, you have the means to do a good deed. Take this for example. Thunderstorms often hit here, yet we don't put up lightning rods.

Dikoi Because they're rubbish.

Kuligin How can they be rubbish if there's been experiments?

Dikoi What kind of lighting rods are these?

Kuligin Steel ones.

Dikoi is in a rage.

Dikoi I see – anything else?

Kuligin Steel rods.

Dikoi is getting more and more angry.

Dikoi I know they're rods. I heard you, you little snake – what else is there? You never shut up about rods. But what else is there?

Kuligin Nothing else.

Dikoi A thunderstorm – what would that be in your opinion? Come on, speak up.

Kuligin Electricity.

Dikoi stomps his foot.

Dikoi What is he babbling about? Elsitricity. And you tell me you're not a thief. Thunderstorms are sent to punish us. We should fear God. But you're trying to get us to defend ourselves with your rods and poles and contraptions. Christ forbid. What are you? A Tartar, is that it? A heathen, eh? Say it out. A Tartar …

Kuligin Your honour, Derzhavin said:
    My body will turn to dust,
    My mind will fight lightning.

Dikoi And for claptrap like that I could send you up before the mayor. He'd give you what you deserve. Hi there, good men, listen to what he has to say.

Kuligin Nothing to be done – I give up, I may as well. When I have my million, then I'll have my say.

Dikoi How will that happen? Thieve it from someone, yes? Stop him. Look at the little peasant, miserable cheat. How can you stay human dealing with people like that? I don't know – I don't.

He turns to the people gathered around.

And as for you, you'd drive anyone to sin, you devil. Here I was not wanting to lose my temper this day, and he has gone and got me in a rage on purpose. May he rot in hell. Has the rain stopped now or what?

Shapkin It seems to have –

Dikoi Seems to? Get out and look, you arsehole. No use thinking.

Shapkin goes out from under the arches.

Shapkin It's stopped.

Dikoi exits and the others follow.
For a few moments the stage is bare.
Varvara quickly enters under the arches. Hiding herself, she peeps out.

SCENE THREE

Varvara It's him I think.

Boris passes at the back of the stage.

You.

He looks round.

Come over here.

She beckons him with her hand and he enters.

Katerina – what are we going to do with her? In Jesus' name, tell me.

Boris What's wrong?

Varvara What's wrong – something awful. Her husband's come home – did you not know? They weren't expecting him, but he's home.

Boris I didn't know.

Varvara She's nearly lost control of herself.

Boris Then I've lived my ten short days while he wasn't here – that's clear. Now I won't even see her.

Varvara Listen to him – how can you talk like that? Now you listen to me. Her whole body is shaking. You'd think she had fever. She's like a ghost. Rushing through the whole house as if she's searching for something. She has the eyes of a mad woman and she's not stopped sobbing. Jesus Christ, what am I to do with her?

Boris She'll pull out of it maybe, you know.

Varvara No, I don't know. She daren't set eyes on her husband. My mother's begun to notice. She's giving looks that could kill her. She watches her like a snake. That just makes her worse. And I'm scared to death.

Boris What have you got to fear?

Varvara You do not know her. To us she is a strange being. With her anything could happen. She could do things that –

Boris Lord God, what *can* we do? Have a sensible chat with her. Can you really not talk her out of it?

Varvara I'm trying. She won't listen to a word. Don't go near her – that's for the best.

Boris What might she do, you think?

Varvara Throw herself at her husband's feet, tell him everything. That's what. That's why I'm scared.

He is alarmed.

Boris She could do that?

Varvara That one could do anything.

Boris Where is she now?

Varvara With himself, walking on the boulevard – Mother's with them. If you want, you go too. No, don't go – that's for the best. She'll lose her head totally.

There are rumbles of thunder in the distance.

Looks like a storm coming.

She looks outside.

Yes, and rain. Here's a crowd of people coming. Bury yourself somewhere – I'll stay where I can be seen. That way they'll make nothing of it.

Several men and women from all stations in life enter. Then Kabanova, Kabanov, Katerina and Kuligin come in.

SCENE FOUR

Katerina rushes in and grabs Varvara tightly by the arm.

Katerina Varvara – Varvara.

Varvara Stop now – what is wrong with you?

Katerina My death – this is it.

Varvara Catch yourself on. Now. Come to your senses.

Katerina I can not. I can do nothing. My heart is hurting me – hurting –

Kabanova People should be prepared to die – that's how to live. They'd have nothing to fear then. That's my way.

Kabanov Mother, exactly what sort of sins could she have committed? She's the same as the rest of us. The woman is nervous, that's all, that's her nature.

Kabanova How do you know? There's always a darkness in people's soul.

He jokes.

Kabanov Well, I've been away, that's true. Now I'm home. There's nothing.

Kabanova Maybe it was when you weren't here.

He jokes again.

Kabanov Come on, Katya. Confess, pet. Better that than if you stay a sinner. You can't hide them from me. You know that. Don't be a bold girl. I know the lot.

She looks into Kabanov's eyes.

Katerina My loved husband.

Varvara Can you not leave the woman alone? Can you not see how rough it's been for her without you?

Boris moves out from the crowd and bows to the Kabanovs.

Katerina No.

Kabanov What's put the fear of God into her? Do you think it was a stranger? This man's a friend of ours. Is your uncle well?

Boris Grand, thank God.

Katerina What more does he want from me? Is it not enough for him that I'm in hell?

She leans against Varvara and sobs.
Varvara speaks loudly, so her mother hears her.

Varvara We've worn ourselves out. What are we to do with this girl – I don't know. Then strangers come and stick their oar in.

She makes a sign to Boris who moves away to the far entrance of the arch.
Kuligin moves out into the middle of the crowd and addresses them.

Kuligin Tell me the truth – just what is it frightens you?
Every blade of grass – every single flower – is enjoying
this. And here we are cowering away as if there were
some kind of catastrophe. Will the storm wipe you
away, is that it? This is not a warning – it's a blessing.
A blessing! But you see harm in everything. When the
Northern Lights begin to shine, admire them – marvel at
God's great wisdom! 'The day breaks in the midnight
lands.' But you're petrified – you can only imagine this
is a sign of war or plague. When a comet arrives, don't
turn your eyes away from it. The beauty of it. We've
been looking up at the stars for so long they're all the
same, but here is something new. Gaze on it, admire it.
You're too terrified even to glance at the sky – look at
the grip fear has got hold on you. My good people –
I am not afraid. Come on, we'll go out.

Boris We will. There's more to fear here than outside.

They exit.

SCENE FIVE

Kabanova What was all that about? God, can that man
ramble on. Better to say nothing than to listen to the like
of that. It's a nice day for us all when we have prophets
like that in our midst. What hope is there for young
people if men his age think that way?

Glasha The whole sky's clouded over. It's like someone's
pulled a shawl on it to hide its face.

Shapkin Look, that cloud's rolling along like a ball –
you'd think there was someone living and twisting inside
it. It's creeping up on us – it really is creeping up – you
would think it was alive.

Townsperson Mark my words, this storm has its evil side. That's the truth, because I know. It will either kill somebody or it will set a house on fire. Wait and see. Look at the colour of that sky – this is not natural.

Katerina What are they saying? They're saying it will kill someone.

Kabanov Pay no heed. They're talking rubbish, saying whatever comes into their head.

Kabanova Don't pass judgement on your elders. They know more than you do. Old people can read all the signs. An old person doesn't throw words to the wind.

Katerina Tisha, I know who the storm will kill.

Varvara speaks quietly to Katerina.

Varvara You be quiet now.

Kabanov How do you know?

Katerina Me – it will kill me. Pray for me. Pray.

The old lady with the footmen enters.
Katerina hides herself with a shriek.

SCENE SIX

Lady Why are you hiding? No use hiding. I can see you're afraid. You don't want to die. Live a little longer, you'd like that. Why should you not? A beautiful girl like you. Look at you. It makes me laugh – beauty. You should pray to God to destroy your beauty. Beauty is our curse. You ruin yourself, you tempt other people, and then just you try enjoying that beauty of yours. So many people you will make sin. Young men without a brain in their heads will fight duels – they'll stab each other with swords. Isn't that a fine thing? Old men who are wise and holy, they forget about death, they're so bewitched by beauty. Who will have to pay for it? *You* will have to pay for everything. Bury that beauty deep down in the water. That's better. Do it now – do it now.

Katerina hides herself.

You silly girl, where can you hide yourself? You can't escape from the sight of God.

A roll of thunder.

You will all burn in the eternal fire.

She exits.

Katerina I am dying.

Varvara Why must you torture yourself? Get into a corner and say a prayer. You'll feel better.

Katerina goes up to the wall and sinks to her knees. She suddenly leaps up.

Katerina Hell – hell – burning fires of hell.

Kabanova, Kabanov and Varvara crowd round her.

My heart's torn to ribbons. I cannot stand it any more. Mother – Tikhon – I have sinned before God and before you. Did I not swear I would look at no man when you were away? Remember that – do you not remember? And do you know what I have done while you weren't here? I am a bad woman. On the very first night I walked out of the house –

In tears, Kabanov becomes distressed and pulls at her sleeve.

Kabanov No need for this – say nothing – no need – what are you doing? Mother's here.

Kabanova speaks harshly.

Kabanova Come on, speak. You've started, so say it all.

Katerina On every one of those ten nights I walked –

Kabanov goes to embrace her.

Kabanova Leave her. Who with?

Varvara She's lying – she doesn't know herself what she's saying.

Kabanova Keep your mouth shut. That's how it was, yes. Come on, who was it with?

Katerina Boris Grigorevich.

There is a roll of thunder.
Katerina wails and falls into Tikhon's arms.

Kabanova Now, son – do you see where freedom leads you? I warned but you would not listen. And now you've got what was coming to you.

Act Five

The same setting as Act One.
  Twilight.
  Kuligin sits on a bench.
  Kabanov approaches along the boulevard.
  Kuligin sings.

Kuligin
  The darkness of night covers the skies
  All people, at rest, have closed their eyes.

  He sees Kabanov.

Kuligin Good evening, sir. Are you walking far?

Kabanov Home. I suppose you've got word about our
bother. The whole house is in chaos.

Kuligin I've heard, sir, I have.

Kabanov Did you hear I went to Moscow? Before I hit
the road, mother delivered a long lecture to me. No
sooner had I set off than I started to let go. I was just
delighted to clear out and do as I pleased. I was not sober
for the whole journey, and in Moscow I was still slugging
drink back – a right bender, I can tell you. I was having
a full year's fun! And I never thought once about home.
Even if I had remembered it, it would not have entered
my head what was being carried on here. You've heard?

Kuligin I've heard, sir.

Kabanov Now, old fella, I'm a mountain of misery.
Ruined – that's what I am, and for nothing, sweet damn
all.

Kuligin Your mother is hard, sir, very hard.

Kabanov She surely is. And she's the source of this.
In God's name tell me what I am being ruined for?
I stopped of at Dikoi's just now. We had a few drinks.
I thought it might improve me, but I felt worse, Kuligin.
What has my wife done to me? There can't be worse –

Kuligin It's a rough business, sir – it's hard to pass
judgement.

Kabanov Come off it. What *is* there worse than this?
Killing isn't enough punishment for this. My mother says
she should be buried alive in the earth. That will slap it
into her. But I do love her. I can't bear to lay a finger on
her. I did knock her about a bit, my mother ordered me.
Then I look at her and my heart breaks – can you fathom
that, Kuligin? My mother's devouring her, and she walks
around like some kind of shadow, like somebody who's
not there. All she does is cry, she's wasting away like
wax. Just looking at her – it's killing me.

Kuligin Would there be no way you could patch things
up in a friendly fashion, sir? Just forgive her and never
mention it again? After all, you yourself are not without
sin.

Kabanov I can confirm that.

Kuligin And see you don't start blaming her when
you've a drink or two taken. She'd be a good wife to
you, sir – you'll see – the best of any of them.

Kabanov Can you get it into your head, Kuligin, if it
were only myself, but there's my mother – no power on
earth would shift her –

Kuligin Then it's high time, sir, you were your own man.

Kabanov What do I do? Rip myself in two, is that it?
They say I haven't a thought of my own. So that means

I have to let someone else do my thinking. I'll go on drinking till I drop, then Mother can baby me like some infant idiot.

Kuligin Rough business, sir, rough business. What about Boris Grigorevich, sir?

Kabanov That good for nothing – he's been sent to the arsehole of nowhere, among the Chinese. His uncle's packed him off to work in an office of some merchant friend he knows. Three years he'll be there.

Kuligin How's he taking that?

Kabanov In a total state – roaring crying. Me and his uncle gave him what for this morning – a right dressing down. He never opened his mouth back at us. You'd think he'd turned into a dumb animal. Do what you want with me, he says, but don't torture her. He feels sorry for her as well.

Kuligin He's a good man, sir.

Kabanov His luggage is packed, the horses are ready. He's a sorry man. It's terrible. I can see he wants to make his farewells to her. Not a snowball's chance in hell. I've had enough. He is my enemy after all, Kuligin. Hung, drawn and quartered, that's what he should get to let him know –

Kuligin We have to forgive our enemies, sir.

Kabanov Run on and tell that to my mother. Hear what she has to answer. Our family has been shattered, Kuligin. We're not like relatives now. We're like enemies. Mother never stopped nagging at Varvara. She wouldn't take it – that's the kind of her. She upped and outed –

Kuligin Where to?

Kabanov Who knows? They say it's with Kudryash, she's done a runner with that Vanya. He can't be seen anywhere either. I'm going to tell you straight, Kuligin, it's mother's fault. She's the one started bullying her – caging her in. 'Don't cage me', she says 'or I'll make worse happen.' And that's exactly what happened. What am I to do now, tell me? Teach me how to live now. My house sickens my stomach. I'm ashamed to meet people. I try to do a bit of work but my hands fail me. I'm going to my home now and do you think I'm heading there a happy man?

Glasha enters.

Glasha Master?

Kabanov What is it?

Glasha Things are bad at home, sir.

Kabanov God almighty, one thing after another, what is it now?

Glasha Your wife –

Kabanov What? Is she dead then?

Glasha No, master. She's wandered off somewhere. We can find her nowhere. We're run off our legs looking.

Kabanov I'll have to go and search for her, Kuligin. My main worry is that she'll harm herself, the terrible state she's in. She's lost her mind, I can't tell you, lost it completely. Your heart breaks just to look at her. Has she been gone long?

Glasha Not that long, master. It's our fault. We didn't keep a close enough eye on her. But what can you say? We couldn't guard her every minute of the day.

Kabanov What are you standing there for? Off you go.

Glasha exits.

You come with me, Kuligin.

They exit.
  For a few moments the stage is empty.
  From the opposite side Katerina enters. She quietly
crosses the stage, as if in a trance, speaking her
soliloquy in a pensive manner, repeating her words.

SCENE TWO

Katerina Nowhere – he's nowhere. No. The poor man.
What is he doing right now? Say goodbye to him – if
I could say goodbye to him – and then die – I may as
well – die then. Such trouble I led him into – why did I?
Nothing's easier after it – nothing. Perish – I should
perish – me alone – should. Ruined myself, ruined him,
ruined, disgrace on myself, I brought it on myself, and
I brought eternal disgrace on him. Eternal.

  Silence.

I wish I could remember. I can't remember what he said.
How he took pity on me.

  She clutches her head.

I can remember nothing. I've forgotten it all. Nights –
the nights are hard for me – so hard. We all go to bed.
I go as well. For them it's nothing. Me, I'm like I'm in
my grave. And in the dark, the dark scares me. Some
kind of noise, singing, they're burying someone. It's so
quiet, so quiet, quiet it's a long way off, a long way from
me. The morning makes you so happy. Light. You don't
want to get up though. Same people, same words, same
torture. Why do they look at me like that? Why don't
they kill people for this these days? Why did they change
things? They used to kill women like me in the old days.
They would have taken me and thrown me in the Volga.
And I would have been delighted. They say if they

punish you, it lifts the sin from you, but if you live, you will suffer for your sin. And I have done enough suffering have I not? How much longer – suffering? What do I live for – what is there now – what? I want nothing. I care for nothing. Not even the light of God. Why does death still not come? No matter what I see, no matter what I hear, no matter – there is nothing but this sore heart here.

She points to her heart.

If I could live with him – live with him – I could see some sort of happiness – but what difference would it make? I've lost my soul already. I miss him – I miss him. And if I can't see you, then at least hear me – you can hear me far away. The winds of the air, wild winds, carry my sorrow to him – I need him. Saints in heaven, I need him – I need him.

She goes up to the bank of the river and calls loudly at the top of her voice.

Joy, life, soul, I love you – answer me.

Boris enters. He does not see Katerina.

SCENE THREE

Boris Dear Christ – that was her voice. Where is she?

He looks around.
She rushes up to him and falls on his neck.

Katerina I've seen you.

She weeps on his chest.
Silence.

Boris At least God's been good to let us weep together.

Katerina You've not forgotten me?

Boris Forget you – how could I?

Katerina No, you couldn't – don't. You're not angry with me?

Boris What is there for me to be angry about?

Katerina Please forgive me. I didn't want to harm you. I could not stop myself. I can't remember what I said or did.

Boris Enough – stop, please.

Katerina How are you? What's going to happen to you?

Boris I'm leaving.

Katerina Where?

Boris A long way away, Katya. Siberia.

Katerina Take me with you.

Boris Katya, I can't. I'm not going there of my free will. Uncle is sending me, the horses are ready. I managed to get away from uncle for a minute. I just wanted to bid farewell to the place where the two of us used to meet.

Katerina God go with you. Don't mourn for me. For a while you'll pine for me, my darling, but then you'll forget.

Boris Why are you worrying about me? I'm a free man. You – what about you? What about your mother-in-law?

Katerina Torments – cages me in – she does – tells everybody, even my husband, 'Don't believe a word that comes from her, that one is cunning.' People troop after me all day. They laugh in my face. And every word is a slap across the mouth.

Boris And your husband?

Katerina One minute kindness itself, the next in a rage with me. He's drinking like a fish. He turns my stomach – he turns my stomach. When he touches me I'd prefer his fist to his fingers' caress.

Boris Our fate's rough, Katya.

Katerina Rough as can be. Dying would be a relief, that's how rough.

Boris Who could have known we would be tortured like this because we love each other? I should have cleared off a long time ago.

Katerina Seeing you was my ruination. I've had little fun in this life, but I've had my fill of suffering. How much more there is of it. But why think of what's to come? I've seen you here, now. That can't be taken from me. I need no more. All I needed was to see you. I feel easier now. It's as if a mountain has been heaved off my shoulders. I kept thinking you were angry with me, you were cursing me.

Boris Don't say that – don't.

Katerina It's not what I mean – not what I'm trying to say. I missed you – I missed you. But now I've seen you.

Boris They must not find us here.

Katerina Stay – I've something I want to say to you – stay. And I've forgotten. Something I needed to say. My head's all confused. I can remember nothing.

Boris It's time, Katya.

Katerina Wait – wait –

Boris What did you want to say?

Katerina I'll tell you in a minute.

She thinks.

I know now. When you're travelling, don't go past any beggars without giving them something. Ask them to pray for my sinful soul.

Boris If these people knew what it takes out of me to say goodbye. This bitter farewell. May they swallow what I'm tasting now. Katya, goodbye.

He embraces her and moves to leave.

Evil monsters – the lot of you. God grant me strength –

Katerina Stay. Let me look at you for the last time – stay. Enough. Now God go with you. Run, quickly, go.

He moves off a few paces and stops.

Boris Something's wrong, Katya. You're not thinking of doing something are you? My road will be a rough one, I'll be tortured thinking of you.

Katerina Nothing. Nothing. God go with you.

He tries to come back to her.

No need. No. Enough.

He is sobbing.

Boris Then God be with you. I ask one thing of God. Let her die soon, let her torment you no longer.

He goes out.
  Katerina follows him with her eyes and remains lost in thought for a short while.

SCENE FOUR

Katerina is alone.

Katerina Where now? Home? No. Home or my grave – one and the same. Home or the grave. The grave, yes.

Better there. A grave under a tree – small – and sweet.
The sun will warm it. Rain will water it. The grass in
spring, soft grass will grow on it. Birds will fly onto the
tree. They'll sing. They'll breed their young. Flowers will
grow: yellow ones, red and blue. All flowers.

She thinks.

All flowers. Quiet, peaceful. I feel better I think. I do not
want to think about life again. Live again? No, I can't,
no. It is hideous. People hate me. The house hates me,
the very walls. I can't go there. And I will not – no. If I
walk back among them, they'll still be gathered around
hissing the same things at me. What is that to me? It's
grown dark. They're singing somewhere. What are they
singing? I can't make it out. Die right now. What are
they singing? All the same to me – whether death comes
to me or I come to death. I cannot go on living. And
that's a sin. They will not pray over me. Whoever loves
me will pray. In the coffin, they cross your arms. Yes
they do, I remember now. But what if they catch me and
haul me home against my will. Run, quick.

She goes up to the river bank and sings loudly.

Love, joy, goodbye.

She goes out.
    *Kabanova, Kabanov, Kuligin and a watchman with
a lantern enter.*

SCENE FIVE

Kuligin They say she was sighted here.

Kabanov You're sure of that?

Kuligin They caught a good look at her.

Kabanov Thank Christ, they saw her alive at least.

Kabanova There you were in a panic. Crying your eyes out. You'll do that time and time again. We'll have good reason to suffer her for a long time yet.

Kabanov What took her to this place? There's people here. Why did she think she could hide herself here?

Kabanova Do you not see what she's up to? She's a cornered rat, but she's still trying to smell her own way out.

People with lanterns gather on all sides.

Townsperson Is she found?

Kabanova Not yet, no. She seems to have vanished somewhere.

Shapkin How did that happen?

Townsperson Where could she have got to?

Glasha She'll show up.

Shapkin We're bound to find her.

Glasha You'll see, she'll be back when she wants to be back.

A voice offstage shouts 'A boat – get a boat.'
From the shore Kuligin calls.

Kuligin Who's shouting? What's wrong?

Voice A woman's flung herself into the water.

Kuligin runs out, followed by several others.

SCENE SIX

Kabanov Christ – it's her – it has to be.

He tries to run off.
Kabanova holds him back by the arm.

Mother, for Jesus sake, let me go. If I don't drag her out, I myself – I will – how can I live without her?

Kabanova Do not ever think that – I do not allow you. Do yourself in because of that one? Is she worth that? Has she not heaped enough shame on our heads? Look what she's dreamt up for us now.

Kabanov Let me go.

Kabanova Enough are there without you as well. If you go, I'll curse you.

He falls to his knees.

Kabanov One look at her – that's all I want.

Kabanova When they haul her out, you'll look at her.

He stands up and speaks to the men.

Kabanov Can you see anything?

Glasha Not a thing – it's pitch dark down there.

Townsperson They're shouting something – I can't make out a word.

Glasha That's Kuligin's voice.

Townsperson They're coming down the bank of the river with lanterns.

Glasha They're coming here – they're carrying her.

Several people come back in from the river.

Shapkin Well done, Kuligin. Quite near she was, lying in one of those deep pockets of water by the bank. You could see by the lantern she was a long way off in the river. He got a glimpse of her dress and pulled her out.

Kabanov Alive – is she –

Shapkin Alive – what do you mean? She threw herself in from the top – she jumped off that cliff up there. She fell onto an anchor and hit herself, poor child. Look, boys, she is as she was living. Just a small wound to her temple, and there's one – just one single drop of blood.

Kabanov rushes forward to be met by Kuligin and a crowd of men carrying Katerina.

SCENE SEVEN

Kuligin Your Katerina. Take her. Do what you want with her. Here's her body. Have it. But her soul is not yours any more. She's now standing before her Maker, and he will show her more mercy than you.

He places her body on the ground and runs out. Kabanov throws himself on Katerina.

Kabanov Katya! Katya!

Kabanova Enough. It's a sin to weep over her likes.

Kabanov Mother, it was you murdered her.

Kabanova What are you saying?

Kabanov You.

Kabanova You remember your manners.

Kabanov You.

Kabanova Have you forgotten –

Kabanov You.

Kabanova Who are you addressing?

Kabanov *You* murdered her. You – you.

Kabanova I will have words at home with you later.

She bows low to the assembled people.

Good people, I thank you for your help.

Everybody bows.

Kabanov Katya, it's all over for you, it's all right. Me, I've been left to live in this world, I've been left to suffer. Why?